COMBATING SPIRITUAL STRONGHOLDS SERIES

Overcoming The Religious Spirit

by Rick Joyner

Published & Distributed By
MorningStar Publications
16000 Lancaster Highway
Charlotte, N

Overcoming
The
Religious Spirit

Table Of Contents

Part I

Discerning The Religious Spirit

Loving God is the greatest commandment, and the greatest gift that we can possess. The second greatest commandment is to love our neighbor. As the Lord affirmed, the whole law is fulfilled by keeping these two commandments. That is, if we keep these two commandments, we will keep the whole law (see Matthew 22:34-40, Romans 13:8).

If we love the Lord, we will not worship idols. If we love our neighbors, we will not envy them, steal from them, murder them, etc. Therefore, keeping these two positive commandments to love will enable us to fulfill all of the negative "do nots" of the law.

Simple love for God will overcome most of the evil in our hearts, and it is the most powerful weapon against evil in the world. Because loving God is our highest goal, it must be the primary focus of our lives. That is why one of the enemy's most deceptive and deadly attacks upon the church is meant to divert us from this ultimate quest. It is his strategy to keep us focused on the evil in our lives, knowing that we will become what we are beholding (see II Corinthians 3:18). As long as we keep looking at the evil, it will continue to have dominion over us. When we look to the Lord and behold His glory, we will be changed into His image.

This is not to imply that we should ignore the sins and errors that are in our lives. In fact, the Scriptures command us to examine ourselves and test ourselves to be sure that we are still in the faith (see II Corinthians 13:5). The issue is what do we do after the iniquity is discovered? Do we turn to the Tree of the Knowledge of Good and Evil, or to the Tree of Life? Do we try to make ourselves better so that we will then be acceptable to God, or do we turn to the cross of Jesus to find both the forgiveness and the power to overcome the sin?

A primary strategy of the enemy is intended to keep us focused on the evil, partaking of the Tree of Knowledge, and away from the glory of the Lord and the cross. This tactic comes in the form of a *religious spirit,* an evil spirit that is the counterfeit of the true love of God and true worship. It has probably done far more damage to the church than have the New Age movement and all other cults combined.

The Nature of a Religious Spirit

A religious spirit is a demon which seeks to substitute religious activity for the power of the Holy Spirit in our lives. Its primary objective is to have the church **"holding to a form of godliness, although they have denied its power" (II Timothy 3:5).** The apostle Paul completed his exhortation with **"*avoid* such men as these."** This religious spirit is the **"leaven of the Pharisees and Sadducees"**

(Matthew 16:6) of which the Lord warned His disciples to beware.

The Lord often used metaphors to illustrate the lessons He taught. The religious spirit does operate like the leaven in bread. It does not add substance or nutritional value to the bread, it only inflates it. Such is the by-product of the religious spirit. It does not add to the life and power of the church, but merely feeds the very pride of man which caused the first fall, and almost every fall since.

Satan seems to understand even better than the church that **"God resists the proud, but gives grace to the humble" (James 4:6 NKJV).** He knows very well that God will not inhabit any work that is inflated with pride, and that God Himself will even resist such a work. So Satan's strategy is to make us proud—even proud of good things, such as how much we read our Bibles, or witness, or feed the poor. He knows that if we do the will of God in pride, our work will be counterproductive and could even ultimately work toward our fall.

Satan also knows that once leaven gets into the bread, it is extremely difficult to remove. Pride, by its very nature, is the most difficult stronghold to remove or correct. A religious spirit keeps us from hearing the voice of God by encouraging us to assume that we already know God's opinion, what He is saying, and what pleases Him. This delusion is the result of believing that God is just like us. This will even cause the rationalization of Scripture, having us believe that rebukes, exhortations and words of correction are for other people, but not for us.

If a religious spirit is a problem in your life, you have probably already begun to think about how badly someone you know needs to read this message. It may not even have occurred to you that God put this into your hands because *you* need it. In fact, we all need it. This is one enemy that all of us are probably battling to some degree. It is imperative that we get free of this devastating deception, and stay free. We will not be able to worship the Lord in Spirit and truth until we do.

The degree to which we have been delivered from this powerful deception will directly affect the degree to which we will be able to preach the true gospel in power. The church's confrontation with the religious spirit will be one of the epic battles of the last days. Everyone will be fighting in this battle. The only issue to be determined is which side we will be on.

We will not have the authority to deliver others from darkness if we are not free from it ourselves. To begin taking ground from this vast enemy, we must ask the Lord to shine His light on us, showing how this applies to us personally. As illustrated by the Lord's continual confrontations with the Pharisees, the church's most desperate fight from the very beginning has been with this spirit. Just as the primary characteristic of the Pharisees was focusing on what was wrong with others while being blind to their own faults, the religious spirit tries to make us do the same.

The Great Deception

One of the most deceptive characteristics about the religious spirit is that it is founded upon zeal for God. We tend to think that zeal for God cannot be evil, but that depends on *why* we are zealous for Him.

Paul wrote of his Jewish brethren in Romans 10:2: **"For I bear them witness that they have a *zeal* for God, but not in accordance with knowledge."** No one on earth prayed more, fasted more, read the Bible more, had a greater hope in the coming of the Messiah, or had more zeal for the things of God than the Pharisees. Yet, they were the greatest opposers of God and His Messiah when He came.

The young Saul of Tarsus was motivated by zeal for God while he was persecuting His church. Zeal for God is one of the most desperately needed characteristics of the church today, most of which is bound by a terrible Laodicean lukewarmness. The Lord commanded the Laodicean church to **"be zealous therefore, and repent"** (Revelation 3:19).

Those who are truly zealous are the most difficult to stop, so the enemy's strategy against them is to push them too far. His first step is to get them to glory in their own zeal. Regardless of how important a gift or characteristic is that we have, if the enemy can get us to take pride in it, he will have us in his snare and will use that gift for evil.

The Lord had little trouble with demons while He walked the earth. They quickly recognized His authority and begged for mercy. It was the conservative, zealous, religious community that immediately became His greatest enemy. Those who were the most zealous for the Word of God crucified the Word Himself when He became flesh to walk among them. The same is still true.

All of the cults and false religions combined have not done as much damage to the moves of God as the opposition, or infiltration, of the religious spirit in the church. Cults and false religions are easily discerned, but the religious spirit has thwarted or diverted possibly every revival or movement to date, and it still retains a seat of honor throughout most of the visible church.

It is a manifestation of the religious spirit that will take its seat in the very temple of God, declaring himself to be God (II Thessalonians 2:4). The temple of God is no longer made with hands, and this is not speaking about a building in Jerusalem. This man of sin will take his seat in *the church.* Unfortunately, it will be the church that allows him to do this.

The Two Foundations

Like most of the enemy's strongholds, the religious spirit builds its work on two basic foundations: fear and pride. *The religious spirit seeks to have us serve the Lord in order to gain His approval, rather than from a position of having received our approval through the cross of Jesus.* Therefore the religious spirit bases relationship to God on personal discipline rather than the propitiatory sacrifice of Christ. The motivation for doing this can be either fear or pride, or a combination of both.

Fear and pride are the two basic results of the Fall, and our deliverance from them is usually a long process. That is why the Lord even gave Jezebel **"time to repent" (see Revelation 2:20-21).** The biblical Jezebel, the wife of King Ahab, was a very religious woman, but she was given to false religion. The Lord gave her time to repent, because the roots of this spirit go so deep that time is required to fully repent and be delivered from it.

However, even though the Lord gave Jezebel time to repent, He rebuked the church of Thyatira for *tolerating* her (verse 20). We can be patient with people who have religious spirits, but we must not tolerate their ministry in our midst while we are waiting! If this spirit is not confronted quickly, it will possibly do more damage to the church, our ministries, our families, and our lives, than any other assault that we may suffer.

The Foundation of Guilt

Eli, the priest who raised Samuel, is a biblical example of someone who ministered in a religious spirit founded upon guilt. Eli had so much zeal for the Lord that when he heard that the Ark had been captured by the Philistines, he fell over and died. He had spent his life trying to serve the Lord as the High Priest, but the very first prophetic word given to Samuel was one of the most frightening rebukes given in the Scriptures—and it was directed to Eli!

For I have told him that I am about to judge his house forever for the iniquity which he knew, because his sons brought a curse on themselves and he did not rebuke them.

And therefore I have sworn to the house of Eli that the iniquity of Eli's house shall not be atoned for by sacrifice or offering forever (I Samuel 3:13-14).

Eli's zeal for the Lord was based on sacrifices and offerings intended to compensate for his irresponsibility as a father. Guilt can spur us on to great zeal for the Lord, and our sacrifices and offerings become an attempt to atone for our failures. This is an affront to the cross, which alone can atone for our guilt. Such zeal will never be acceptable to the Lord, even if we could make sacrifices forever.

We should note here that the Lord never said that Eli's sin couldn't be forgiven. He just said that Eli's attempts to atone for sin *by sacrifice and offering* would never succeed. There are multitudes of men and women whose zeal for the Lord is likewise based on an attempt to atone for sin, failure or irresponsibility in other areas of their lives. But all the sacrifices in the world will not atone for even our smallest failure. To even make such an attempt is an insult to the cross of Jesus, which is the only acceptable sacrifice to the Father for sin.

Attempting to gain God's approval by our own sacrifice opens the door wide for a religious spirit, because such service is not based on the blood of Jesus, but on an attempt to make our own atonement for sin. This doesn't mean we should not do things to please the Lord, but we must keep as our motive to be pleasing to the Lord for His joy, not for our acceptance. One is God-centered; the other is self-centered. And this is self-centeredness of the most destructive kind—an attempt to circumvent the cross.

It is also noteworthy that one of the sins of Eli's sons was that they **"despised the offering of the Lord" (I Samuel 2:17).** They appropriated for their own selfish use the sacrifices and offerings brought to the Lord. Those who are gripped by this form of a religious spirit will often be the most zealous to preach the cross, but herein lies the perversion: It emphasizes *their* cross more than the cross of Jesus. Their delight really is more in self-abasement than in the cross of Christ, which alone makes us righteous and acceptable to God.

The Foundation of Pride

Idealism is one of the most deceptive and destructive disguises of the religious spirit. Idealism is of human origin, and is a form of humanism. Although it has the appearance of seeking only the highest standards and the preservation of God's glory, idealism is possibly the most deadly enemy of true revelation and true grace. It is deadly because it does not allow for growing up into grace and wisdom, but attacks and destroys the foundation of those who are in pursuit of God's glory, but are not yet there.

Idealism makes us try to impose on others standards that are beyond what God has required or given the grace for at that time. For example, men controlled by this kind of religious spirit may condemn those who are not praying two hours a day as they are. The truth is, it may be God's will for us to be praying that much, but how we get there is crucial. The grace of God may first call us to pray just ten minutes a day. Then, as we become so blessed by His presence, we will want to spend more and more time with Him until we will not want to quit after ten minutes, then an hour, then two. When we eventually are praying two hours a day, it will be because of our love for prayer and the presence of the Lord, not out of fear or pride.

A person with a religious spirit based on idealism will usually seek the perfect church, and will refuse to be a part of anything less. Those led by the Holy Spirit may also have high hopes for a church, but will still be able to give themselves in service to even some of the most lowly works, in order to help those works grow in vision and maturity. The Holy Spirit is called **"the Helper,"** and those who are truly led by the Spirit will always be looking for ways to help, not just to stand aloof and criticize.

When a religious spirit is founded upon pride, it is evidenced by *perfectionism*. The perfectionist sees everything as black or white. This develops into extremes, requiring that every person and every teaching be judged as either 100% right or 100% wrong. This is a standard with which only Jesus could comply; it will lead to a serious delusion when we impose it on ourselves or others. True grace imparts a truth that sets people free, showing them the way out of their sin, and beckoning them to higher levels of spiritual maturity.

One with a religious spirit can usually point to problems with great accuracy, but seldom has solutions, except to tear down what has already been built. This is the strategy of the enemy to nullify progress that is being made and to sow a discouragement that will limit future progress. This produces the mentality that, if we cannot go straight to the top of the mountain, we should not climb at all, but just "die to self." This is a death that God has not required, and it is a perversion of the exhortation for us to take up our crosses daily.

The perfectionist both imposes and tries to live by standards that stifle true maturity and growth. The grace of God will lead us up the mountain step by step. The Lord does not condemn us because we may trip a few times while trying to climb. He graciously picks us up with the encouragement that we can make it. We must have a vision of making it to the top, and should never condemn ourselves for not being there yet, *as long as we are still climbing*.

James said, **"We all stumble in many ways" (James 3:2).** If we had to wait until we were perfect before we could minister, *no one* would ever qualify for the ministry. Even though perfect obedience and understanding should always be our goal, such will never be found within ourselves, but only as we come to perfectly abide in the Perfect One.

Because we now see **"through a glass darkly" (I Corinthians 13:12 KJV),** or in part, we must always be open to greater accuracy in our beliefs and teachings. One of the greatest delusions of all is that we are already complete in our understanding, or 100% accurate in our perceptions or actions. Those with a religious spirit will usually claim to be open to more understanding, but most of the time this is done to get *everyone else* to be open to what they teach, while they remain steadfastly closed to others.

Jesus blessed Peter and turned the keys of the kingdom over to him just before He had to rebuke him by calling him **"Satan" (see Matthew 16:23).** Right after this greatest of blessings, the enemy deceived him, yet the Lord did not take the keys away from Peter!

In fact, Jesus knew when He gave the keys to Peter that he was soon to deny even knowing Him.

Many years after Peter used the keys to open the door of faith for both the Jews and Gentiles, **"the least of the apostles,"** Paul, had to rebuke him publicly because of his hypocrisy (see I Corinthians 15:9, Galatians 2:11-14). Even so, Peter was promised that he would sit on one of the twelve thrones judging the twelve tribes of Israel (Matthew 19:28). The Lord has proven that He will commission and use men long before most of us would, and when He calls us, He already knows all the mistakes that we will make.

It seems that the Lord's leadership style was to provide a place where his followers could make mistakes and learn from them. If we required our children to be perfectly mature while they were still children, it would stifle their growth and maturity. The same is true in the church. We must correct mistakes, because that is how we learn, but it must be a correction that encourages and frees, not one that condemns and crushes initiative.

The Deadly Combination

One of the most powerful and deceptive forms of the religious spirit is built upon the foundations of both fear and pride. Those who are bound in this way go through periods of deep anguish and remorse at their failures, but this false repentance results only in more self-abasement, and further attempts to make sacrifices that will appease the Lord. Those bound by a religious spirit then often flip to the other side, where they become so convinced that they are superior to other Christians or other groups that they become unteachable and unable to receive reproof. The foundation that they stand on at any given time will be dictated more by external pressure than by true conviction.

Such a religious spirit is so slippery that it will wiggle out of almost any attempt to confront it. If you address the pride, the fears and insecurities will rise up to attract sympathy. If you confront the fear, it will then change into religious pride masquerading as faith. This type of spirit will drive individuals or congregations to such extremes that they will inevitably disintegrate.

The Counterfeit Gift of Discernment

A religious spirit will usually give a counterfeit gift of discernment of spirits. This counterfeit gift thrives on seeing what is wrong with others rather than seeing what God is doing so we can help them along. This is how a religious spirit does some of its greatest damage to the church. Its ministry will almost always leave more damage and division than healing and reconciliation. Its wisdom is rooted in the Tree of the Knowledge of Good and Evil, and though the truth may be accurate, it is ministered in a spirit that kills.

This counterfeit gift of discernment is motivated by suspicion and fear. The suspicion is rooted in such things as rejection, territorial preservation, or general insecurity. The true gift of discernment can only function through love. Any motive other than love will distort spiritual perception. Whenever someone submits a judgment or criticism about another person or group, we should disregard it unless we know that the one bringing it truly loves that person or group, and has an "investment" of service to them.

Angels of Light

When Paul warned the Corinthians about those who ministered in a religious spirit, which sought to bring a yoke of legalism upon the young church, he explained that:

> **Such men are false apostles, deceitful workers, disguising themselves as apostles of Christ.**
>
> **And no wonder, for even Satan disguises himself as an angel of light.**

Therefore it is not surprising if his servants also disguise themselves as servants of righteousness (II Corinthians 11:13-15).

This phrase **"angel of light"** could be interpreted as a "messenger of truth." Satan's most deceptive and deadly disguise is to come as a servant of righteousness, using truths for the purpose of destruction. He is quite skillful at quoting Scripture and using wisdom, but it is the wisdom of the Tree of Knowledge—wisdom that kills. He can accurately point out what is wrong with someone else, but he always does it in such a way that tears down, not offering solutions that lead to deliverance and life.

"Angels of light," who are empowered by a religious spirit, will first look for what is wrong with someone rather than for what is right. Although this spirit usually comes in the guise of protecting the sheep, the truth, or the Lord's glory, it is an evil, critical spirit that will always end up causing division and destruction.

Criticism gives an appearance of wisdom, but it is pride in one of its most base forms. When we criticize someone, we are in effect declaring ourselves to be better than them. We may be better than others in some areas, but if we are, it is only by grace. Believers who recognize the true grace of God never look for ways to put others down, but rather find ways to build them up. As an old proverb declares, "Any jackass can kick a barn down, but it requires a skillful carpenter to build one."

The Religious Spirit and Murder

When Adam and Eve chose to live by the Knowledge of Good and Evil, they were partaking of the religious spirit. The first result of this was self-centeredness—they started looking at themselves. The first child born to them after partaking of this fruit was Cain, who is the first biblical model of a man controlled by the religious spirit.

Cain was **"a tiller of the ground" (Genesis 4:2),** or earthly-minded. The religious spirit will always seek to keep us focused on the earthly realm rather than the heavenly realm. This "seed of Cain" judges by what is seen, and cannot understand those who **"endured, as seeing Him who is unseen" (Hebrews 11:27).**

In Revelation 13:11, we see the second beast **"coming up *out of the earth."*** This is because the spiritual seed of Cain are tillers of the ground. This earthly-mindedness has produced one of the most evil beasts the world will ever know.

Cain also tried to make an offering to the Lord from his own labors. God rejected that sacrifice, but accepted Abel's sacrifice of blood.

24

The fruit of our labors will never be an acceptable offering to the Lord. This was a statement from the beginning that God would only accept the blood of the Lamb. Instead of receiving this correction and repenting, Cain became jealous of his brother and killed him. Those who attempt to live by their own works will often become enraged at those who take their stand on the righteousness of the Lamb.

That is why Saul of Tarsus, the Pharisee of Pharisees, was so enraged against Christians. They represented the greatest threat to that on which the Pharisees had built their whole lives. Because of this, the Pharisees could not endure the very existence of the Christians. Religions that are based on works will easily become violent. This includes "Christian" sects where a doctrine of works has supplanted the cross of Christ.

The Lord said that if a man hates his brother, he is guilty of murder (Matthew 5:21-22). Those who are driven by religious spirits may well try to destroy people by means other than the physical taking of their lives. Many of the onslaughts of slander instigated against churches and ministries are the ragings of this same religious spirit that caused Cain to slay his brother.

The Test of a True Messenger

In Ezekiel 37 the prophet was taken to a valley full of dry bones and asked if they could live. The Lord then commanded him to **"prophesy to the bones."** As he prophesied, they came together, came to life, and then became a great army.

This is an important test which every true ministry must pass. The true prophet can see a great army in even the driest of bones. He will prophesy life to those bones until they come to life and then become an army. A false prophet with a religious spirit will do little more than just tell the bones how dry they are, heaping discouragement and condemnation on them, but imparting no life or power to overcome their circumstances.

Apostles and prophets are given authority to build up and tear down, but we have no right to tear down if we have not first built up. We should give no one the authority to bring correction to the people under our care unless they first have a history of providing spiritual nourishment and building people up. Some may say that such a policy would eliminate the ministry of the prophets altogether, but I say that so-called "prophets" who do not have a heart to build people up *should be* eliminated from ministry. As Jude said of them, **"These are grumblers, fault**

26

finders" who are **"hidden reefs in your love feasts"** (see Jude 11-16).

Even so, as we can see from Eli's tragic example, woe to the shepherds who feed and care for the sheep, but fail to *correct* them. The true grace of God is found between the extremes of unrighteous faultfinding and unsanctified mercy (approving of things that God condemns). Either extreme can be the result of a religious spirit.

Part II

Masks Of The
Religious Spirit

The Spirit of Jezebel

The spirit of Jezebel is a form of the religious spirit. Just as Jezebel was the ambitious and manipulative wife of King Ahab—a weak leader who allowed her to dictate policy in his kingdom—the Jezebel spirit will usually be found supplanting weak leadership. The Jezebel spirit usually gains its dominion by making political alliances, and often it uses a deceptively humble and submissive demeanor in order to manipulate. However, once this spirit gains authority, it will usually manifest a strong control spirit and shameless presumption. Despite its name, this spiritual problem is not limited to women.

Jezebel **"calls herself a prophetess" (Revelation 2:20).** This is often one of the telltale signs of false prophets who are operating in a religious spirit—they are preoccupied with their own recognition. To the degree that self-seeking and the need for recognition abides within us, our ministry will be corrupted. Those who are easily offended because they are not given an important title or position should never be accepted by that title or given that position! The difference between those motivated by a desire for recognition and those motivated by love for the Lord is the difference between the false prophet and the true. The Lord Himself declared:

He who speaks from himself *seeks his own glory* **[literally: "recognition"]; but He who is seeking the glory of the one who sent Him, He is true, and there is no unrighteousness in Him (John 7:18).**

Demanding recognition for herself, Jezebel serves as the enemy of the true prophetic ministry. Jezebel was the greatest enemy of one of the Old Covenant's most powerful prophets, Elijah, whose ministry especially typified preparing of the way for the Lord. The Jezebel spirit is one of the most potent forms of the religious spirit, which seeks to keep the church and the world from being prepared for the return of the Lord.

The Jezebel spirit especially attacks the prophetic ministry, because that ministry has an important place in preparing the way for the Lord. That is why John the Baptist was persecuted by a personification of Jezebel, in the wife of Herod. The prophetic ministry is the primary vehicle through which the Lord gives timely, strategic direction to His people. Jezebel knows that removing the true prophets will make the people vulnerable to her false prophets, always resulting in idolatry and spiritual adultery.

When there is a void of hearing the true voice of the Lord, the people will be much more susceptible to the deceptions of the enemy. This is why Jesus called the religious

leaders of His own day **"blind guides"
(Matthew 23:16).** These men, who knew the
messianic prophecies better than anyone else
in the world, looked into the face of the One
who perfectly fulfilled those prophecies and
thought that He was sent from Beelzebub.

Jezebel's prophets of Baal were also given
to sacrifice, even to the point of cutting and
flailing themselves while seeking the manifestation of their god. A primary strategy of the
religious spirit is to get the church devoted to
"sacrifice" in a way that perverts the command
for us to take up our crosses daily. This
perversion will have us putting more faith in
our sacrifices than in the Lord's sacrifice. It
will also use sacrifices and offerings to pressure
God to manifest Himself. This is a form of the
terrible delusion that we can somehow
purchase the grace and presence of God with
our good works.

The Root of Self-Righteousness

We do not crucify ourselves for the sake of
righteousness, purification, spiritual maturity, or to get the Lord to manifest Himself;
this is nothing less than conjuring. We are
"crucified with Christ" (Galatians 2:20). If
we "crucify ourselves," it will only result in
self-righteousness—which is pride in one of
its most base forms. This pride is deceptive,
because it gives the appearance of wisdom

and righteousness, of which the apostle Paul warned:

> **Let no one keep defrauding you of your prize by delighting in self-abasement and the worship of the angels, taking his stand on visions he has seen, inflated without cause by his fleshly mind,**
>
> **and not holding fast to the head, from whom the entire body, being supplied and held together by the joints and ligaments, grows with a growth which is from God.**
>
> **If you have died with Christ to the elementary principles of the world, why, as if you were living in the world, do you submit yourself to decrees, such as,**
>
> **"Do not handle, do not taste, do not touch!"**
>
> **(which all refer to things destined to perish with the using)—in accordance with the commandments and teachings of men?**
>
> **These are matters which have, to be sure, the appearance of wisdom in self-made religion and self-abasement and severe treatment of the body, but are of no value against fleshly indulgence (Colossians 2:18-23).**

The religious spirit will make us feel very good about our spiritual condition as long as it is self-centered and self-seeking. Pride feels good; it can even be exhilarating. But it keeps all of our attention on how well we are doing and on how we stand compared to others—not on the glory of God. This results in our putting confidence in discipline and personal sacrifice rather than in the Lord and His sacrifice.

Of course, discipline and a commitment to self-sacrifice are essential qualities for every believer to have. But it is the motivation behind them that determines whether we are being driven by a religious spirit or by the Holy Spirit. A religious spirit motivates through fear and guilt, or through pride and ambition. The motivation of the Holy Spirit is love for the Son of God.

Delighting in self-abasement is a sure symptom of the religious spirit. This does not mean that we can neglect to discipline ourselves, fast, or buffet our bodies as Paul did. However, the problem comes when we take a perverse delight in this, rather than delighting in the Son of God.

Deceptive Revelation

Colossians 2:18-19 indicates that a person with a religious spirit will tend to delight in self-abasement and will often be given to worshiping angels or taking improper stands on visions he has seen. A religious spirit wants us to worship anything or anyone but Jesus. The same spirit that is given to worshiping angels will also be prone to excessively exalting people.

We must beware of anyone who unduly exalts angels or men and women of God, or anyone who uses the visions he has received in order to gain improper influence in the church. God does not give us revelations so that people will respect us more, or to prove our ministry. The fruit of true revelation will be humility, not pride.

Of course, the Scriptures teach that Christians do have these prophetic experiences, and we are also told in Acts 2:17 that they will increase in the last days. Jesus also warned that in the last days there would be many false prophets (Matthew 24:11). Prophetic revelation that is truly from God is crucial to the body of Christ. The enemy knows this very well, which is why he will raise up many false prophets. But they can be easily discerned. As Paul warned the Colossians, the danger doesn't come from those who are *having* prophetic revelations, but from those who have been *inflated* by them.

A religious spirit will always feed our fear or pride, whereas genuine spiritual maturity will always lead to increasing humility. This progression of humility is wonderfully demonstrated in the life of Paul the apostle. In his letter to the Galatians, estimated to have been written in A.D. 56, he declared that when he visited the original apostles in Jerusalem, they **"contributed nothing to me"** (Galatians 2:6). He was by this declaring that he had as much as they did.

In Paul's first letter to the Corinthians, written about six years later, he called himself the **"least of the apostles"** (15:9). In Ephesians 3:8, written in about A.D. 61, he declared himself to be the **"the very least of all saints."** When writing to Timothy in approximately A.D. 65, Paul declared himself to be the **"foremost of all sinners"** (I Timothy 1:15), adding that he had found mercy. *A true revelation of God's mercy is a great antidote for the religious spirit.*

It is clear by this that the great apostle was not completely free of pride in the first years of his ministry. Which of us can claim to be free of it either? However, we are all hopefully growing in grace and, therefore, humility.

Young apostles may exude a lot of pride, but they can still be true apostles. The key here is in which direction we are going. Are we being puffed up by our revelations, our commission, or our accomplishments? Or are we growing in grace and humility?

The Martyr Syndrome

When combined with the religious spirit, the martyr syndrome is one of the ultimate and most deadly delusions. To be a true martyr for the faith and literally lose our life for the sake of Christ is one of the greatest honors that we can receive in this life. Yet, when this is perverted, it is a most tragic form of deception.

When a religious spirit is combined with the martyr syndrome, it is almost impossible for that person to be delivered from the deception that he is "suffering for the gospel." At this point, any rejection or correction received from others is perceived as the price he must pay to "stand for the truth." This warped perspective will drive him even further from the truth and any possibility of correction.

The martyr syndrome can also be a manifestation of the spirit of suicide. It is sometimes easier to "die for the Lord" than it is to live for Him. Those who have a perverted understanding of the cross glory more in death than they do in life. They fail to see that the point of the cross is the resurrection, not the grave.

Self-Help Psychology

There is a "self-help psychology" move-ment that is attempting to replace the power of the cross in the church. Humanisti-cally-based psychology is **"a different gospel" (II Corinthians 11:4);** it is an enemy of the cross, and is another form of the religious spirit. Paul warned us:

As you therefore have received Christ Jesus the Lord, so walk in Him,

having been firmly rooted and now being built up in Him, and established in your faith, just as you were instructed, and overflowing with gratitude.

See to it that no one takes you captive through philosophy and empty deception, according to the tradition of men, according to the elementary principles of the world, rather than according to Christ (Colossians 2:6-8).

We all need "inner healing" to some degree, but much of what is being called inner healing is nothing less than digging up the "old man" and trying to get him healed. The answer to these deep wounds is not a procedure or a formula, but simple forgiveness. When we go to the cross and find forgiveness and true acceptance based on the blood of Jesus, we will find a perfect love able to cast out all of our fears and wash away all bitterness and resentment.

This seems too simple, but that is why Paul said: **"I am afraid, lest as the serpent deceived Eve by his craftiness, your minds should be led astray from the simplicity and purity of devotion to Christ"** (II Corinthians

11:3). Salvation is simple. Deliverance is simple. Yet there is a major strategy of the enemy to dilute the power of the gospel by having us add to it, which is how Eve was deceived. We add to it because we just do not think it will be acceptable unless it somehow seems brilliant or abstract. That is precisely why we must become like children to enter the kingdom.

The Lord commanded the man and woman not to eat from the Tree of the Knowledge of Good and Evil because they would die. When the serpent asked about this command, Eve replied that they could not eat from the tree *"or touch it"* **(Genesis 3:3)**. However, the Lord had not said anything about refraining from touching the tree.

Adding to God's commandments is just as destructive as taking away from them. Anyone who thinks that he can so flippantly add to the Word of God does not respect it enough to keep it when the testing comes. If Satan can get us to either add or subtract from the Word, he then knows our fall is imminent, just like it was for Eve.

Although there are many "Christian" philosophies and therapies that seem wise, most are in fact attempting to be substitutes for the Holy Spirit in our lives. Some people do need counseling, and there are outstanding Christian counselors who do lead people to the cross. But others are simply leading people into a black hole of self-centeredness that will consume them and try to suck in everyone else around them, too. In spite of the Christian terminology, this philosophy is an enemy of the cross of Christ.

Part III

Summary

The Warning Signs of a Religious Spirit

The following is a list of some of the more obvious warning signs of the religious spirit. As stated, almost everyone is battling the religious spirit to at least some degree, and everyone's fight is somewhat different. One may be dealing with all the issues listed below to a small degree, and yet be more free from the yoke of the religious spirit than one who is free of most of these problems, but who has serious problems with just a couple of them.

Our goal must be to get completely free of any influence from the religious spirit by being completely submitted to the Holy Spirit. Without this complete submission to the Lord, there is no way to be free from the religious spirit.

People with a religious spirit:

1. *Will often see their primary mission as the tearing down of whatever they believe is wrong.* Such a person's ministry will result more in division and destruction than in lasting works that are bearing fruit for the kingdom.

2. *Will be unable to accept a rebuke, especially from those they judge to be less spiritual than themselves.* Think back on how *you* responded the last few times someone tried to correct you.

3. *Will have a philosophy that, "I will not listen to people, but only to God."* Since God frequently speaks through people, this is an obvious delusion, revealing serious spiritual pride.

4. *Will be inclined to see more of what is wrong with other people, other churches, etc., than what is right with them.* From the valley John saw Babylon, but when he was carried to a high mountain, he saw the New Jerusalem (Revelation 21:10). If we are only seeing Babylon, it is because of our perspective. Those who are in a place of true vision will have their attention on what God is doing, not men.

5. *Will be subject to an overwhelming feeling of guilt that they can never measure up to the Lord's standards.* This is a root of the religious spirit because it causes us to base our relationship with Him on our performance rather than on the cross. Jesus has already measured up for us; He is the completed work that the Father is seeking to accomplish within us. Our whole goal in life should be simply to abide in Him.

6. *Will keep score on their spiritual life.* This includes feeling better about ourselves because we go to more meetings, read our Bibles more, do more things for the Lord, etc. These are all noble endeavors, but the true measure of spiritual maturity is getting closer to the Lord.

7. *Will believe that they have been appointed to fix everyone else.* These persons become the self-appointed watchmen, or sheriffs, in God's kingdom. They are seldom involved in building, but serve only to keep the church in a state of annoyance and agitation, if not causing serious divisions.

8. *Will have a leadership style which is bossy, overbearing and intolerant of the weakness or failure of others.* James said: **"But the wisdom from above is first pure, then peaceable, gentle, reasonable, full of mercy and good fruits, unwavering, without hypocrisy. And the seed whose fruit is righteousness is sown in peace by those who make peace" (James 3:17-18).**

9. *Will have a sense that they are closer to God than other people, or that their lives or ministries are more pleasing to Him.* This is a symptom of the profound delusion that we draw closer to God because of who we are, rather than through Jesus.

10. *Will take pride in their spiritual maturity and discipline, especially as compared to others.* True spiritual maturity involves growing up into Christ. When we begin to compare ourselves to others, it is obvious that we have lost sight of the true goal—Jesus.

11. *Will believe that they are on the "cutting edge" of what God is doing.* This includes

thinking that we are involved in the most important thing that God is doing.

12. *Will have a mechanical prayer life.* When we start feeling relief when our prayer time is over or we have prayed through our prayer list, we should consider our condition. We will never feel relief when our conversations are over with the one we love.

13. *Will do things in order to be noticed by people.* This is a symptom of the idolatry of fearing people more than we fear God, which results in a religion that serves men instead of God.

14. *Will be overly repulsed by emotionalism.* When people who are subject to a religious spirit encounter the true life of God, it will usually appear to them to be excessive, emotional and carnal. True passion for God is often emotional and demonstrative, such as David exemplified when he brought the ark of God into Jerusalem (see II Samuel 6:14-16).

15. *Will use emotionalism as a substitute for the work of the Holy Spirit.* This seems contradictory to the previous point, but the religious spirit will often take contradictory positions in its drive for self-preservation and exaltation. This use of emotionalism would include such things as requiring weeping and wailing as evidence of repentance, or "falling under the power" as evidence that one has

been touched by God. Both of these can be evidences of the true work of the Holy Spirit; it is when we *require* these manifestations that we are beginning to move in another spirit.

During the First Great Awakening, Jonathan Edwards' meetings would often have some of the toughest, most rebellious men falling to the ground and staying there for up to 24 hours. They got up changed, and such strange manifestations of the Holy Spirit fueled the Great Awakenings. Even so, Edwards stated that people faking the manifestations did more to bring an end to the Great Awakening than the enemies of the revival!

16. *Will be encouraged when their ministries look better than others.* We could include in this being discouraged when it seems that others are looking better or growing faster than we are.

17. *Will glory more in what God did in the past than in what He is doing in the present.* God has not changed; He is the same yesterday, today and forever. The veil has been removed, and we can be as close to God today as anyone ever has been in the past. A religious spirit will always seek to focus our attention on works and on making comparisons, rather than on simply drawing closer to the Lord.

18. *Will tend to be suspicious of, or to oppose, new movements, churches, etc.* This is an obvious

symptom of jealousy, a primary fruit of the religious spirit, or the pride that asserts that God would not do anything new without doing it through us. Of course, those with such a mentality are seldom used by the Lord to birth new works.

19. *Will tend to reject spiritual manifestations that they do not understand.* This is a symptom of the pride and arrogance of presuming that our opinions are the same as God's. True humility keeps us teachable and open, patiently waiting for fruit before making judgments. True discernment enables us to look for and hope for the best, not the worst. For this reason, we are exhorted to **"examine everything carefully; hold fast to that which is good [not what is bad]" (I Thessalonians 5:21).**

20. *Will overreact to carnality in the church.* The truth is, there is probably far more carnality in the church, and a lot less of the Holy Spirit, than even the most critical person has guessed. It is important that we learn to discern between them in order to be delivered from our carnality and grow in our submission to the Holy Spirit. But the critical person will annihilate those who may still be 60% carnal, but were 95% carnal last year. Instead, we need to recognize that people are making progress, and do what we can to help them along the way.

21. *Will overreact to immaturity in the church.* There is an immaturity that is acceptable to the Lord. My two-year-old is immature when compared to my nine- year-old, but that is to be expected. In fact, he may be very mature for a two-year-old. The idealistic religious spirit only sees the immaturity, without considering the other important factors.

22. *Will be overly prone to view supernatural manifestations as evidence of God's approval.* This is just another form of keeping score and comparing ourselves with others. Some of Jesus' greatest miracles, such as walking on water, were seen by only a few. He was doing His works to glorify the Father, not Himself. Those who use the evidence of miracles to promote and build their own ministries and reputations have made a serious departure from the path of life.

23. *Will be unable to join anything that they do not deem perfect or nearly perfect.* The Lord joined, and even gave His life for, the fallen human race. Such is the nature of those who abide in Him.

24. *Will be overly paranoid of the religious spirit.* We do not get free of something by fearing it, but by overcoming it with faith in Christ Jesus.

25. *Will have the tendency to glory in anything but the cross of Jesus, what He has accomplished,*

and who He is. If we are building our lives, ministries or churches on anything but these, we are building on a shaky foundation that will not stand.

Scoring on the Test

We are probably all subject to the religious spirit to at least some degree. Paul exhorted: **"Test yourselves to see if you are in the faith" (II Corinthians 13:5).** First, He did not say to "test your neighbor" or to "test your pastor," but to test *"yourselves."* Using this test to measure others can be a symptom that *we* have a serious problem. If this chapter has given you illumination about problems in another person or ministry, be sure that you respond in the Holy Spirit, heeding Paul's warning to the Galatians:

> **Brethren, even if a man is caught in any trespass, you who are spiritual restore such a one in a spirit of gentleness; each one looking to yourself, lest you too be tempted (Galatians 6:1).**

Ten Things We Can Do To Get Free Of The Religious Spirit

I have been somewhat reticent to try to formulate this list for obvious reasons those who are bound by a religious spirit may tend to interpret this list in a manner that just promotes more religious activity, in place of true intimacy with the Lord. However, I trust that if you have the humility to read this, the Lord will give you His grace to use this list properly, as suggested guidelines to help us draw closer to Him.

1) Develop a secret relationship with the Lord. The Lord warned His disciples not to be like the Pharisees who did their works to be noticed by men, but to do their works in secret before the Father. In this way we begin to put our hope and trust in our relationship to Him, not men. There is no greater security than to know that we are known by God. As the Lord warned, **"How can you believe when you receive glory one from another, but do not seek the glory that is from the one and only true God" (John 5:44).** Seeking glory, or recognition, from men is probably the most destructive thing that we can do to true faith.

2) Pray that the same love with which the Father loved the Son would be in us. The Lord Jesus Himself prayed for the same love with which the Father loved Him to be in us (John 17:). We know that this prayer of the Son of God, who was in perfect harmony with the Father will be answered, but we have not because we ask not. When this love replaces religious duty, our good works will greatly exceed what they would be otherwise.

3) "Study to show yourselves approved unto to God [not men]" (II Timothy 2:15). When we study the word of God in order to show demonstrate our knowledge before men, or to prove our position before men, we have departed from the Spirit of Truth that leads to truth. The Spirit of Truth came to reveal Jesus, not us. We must study His word in order to seek Him, and to do what is approved of Him, not men. As the Lord warned the Pharisees, **"You are those who justify yourselves in the sight of men, but God knows your hearts, for that which is highly esteemed with men is detestable in the sight of God".** If we are motivated to do the things that are highly esteemed with men, or to justify ourselves before men, we will be doing that which is detestable in God's sight.

4) Spend quality time alone with the Lord each day. Endeavor, as much as it is possible, to increase this to the place where you spend more time alone with the Lord than with any other individual. When we are spending time with Him continually we will not be so prone to the guilt that drives us to start measuring our spiritual lives by our works.

5) Seek to hear the voice of the Lord every day. The Lord's sheep know His voice (see John 10:27). They know His voice because they spend time with Him. If a good earthly parent seeks to spend some quality time with their children each day, how much more does the Lord seek to spend quality time with us. That quality of the time can be measured by the quality of the communication. The Lord really does want to speak to all of us each day. If we would refuse to go to bed until we have heard from Him in some meaningful way, our lives would be quickly changed. The most important thing that we can do each day is to spend time with Him, and hear from Him. But do not just seek to hear the words of the Lord, but the Word Himself.

6) Ask the Lord to give us the love for our neighbors that He has for them. Only then will our witness and our ministry to them be pure. But we must always endeavor to love the Lord first, and most. If we love the Lord more than we do our children, or our neighbors, we will love them more than we would otherwise.

7) Seek to turn your criticisms into intercession. Let your first response to seeing something wrong with someone else be to pray for them, asking for grace on their behalf. If someone especially irritates you, endeavor to pray for them even more. If you make an investment in them in prayer, **"where you treasure is there will your heart be also,"** and you will start to genuinely love them. True spiritual authority is founded on love, so if you love them enough the Lord may be able to trust you with the ministry of truth that will set them free. Some of the greatest spiritual victories that are counted in heaven are the ones that turn enemies into friends, which turn those who dwell in darkness into children of the light. This must always be our goal.

8) Continually ask the Lord to see His glory. It is by seeing His glory with an unveiled face that we are changed into His same image (II Corinthians 3:17). Understanding doctrine is important, but until we see His glory it only remains doctrine. When we behold Him the doctrine will become our nature. It is not by believing in our minds, but in our hearts, that it results in righteousness.

9) Keep as one of your highest goals to manifest the sweet aroma of the knowledge of God in every place. Like Moses, ask the Lord not to send you anywhere that His manifest presence is not going to go with you. We should only want to be where He is. And we should always behave as is befitting being in the presence of the King.

10) *When you have failed to do any of these properly, ask forgiveness and "forgetting what lies behind, press on toward the high calling of God in Christ Jesus" (Philippians 3:14 KJV).*

Conclusion

Basically, the religious spirit seeks to replace the Holy Spirit as the source of spiritual life. It does this by seeking to replace true repentance, which leads to grace, with a repentance based on our performance. The effect of this is to replace true humility with pride.

True religion is based on loving the Lord and then loving our neighbors. True religion will promote discipline and obedience, but these are founded on love for the Lord rather than the need or desire for recognition or acceptance. The wife who keeps herself in shape because she loves her husband will be easily distinguished from the one who does it because of her own ego. The former will carry her beauty with grace and dignity; the latter may be physically appealing, but it will be a seductive appeal that is a perversion of true love.

The religious spirit is basically a manifestation of the "good" side of the Tree of the Knowledge of Good and Evil. When Adam and Eve ate of that tree in the Garden, the first result was that they looked at themselves. Self-centeredness is the poison that made that fruit deadly, and it is still the most deadly poison the serpent seeks to give us. In contrast with the religious spirit—which causes us to focus our attention on ourselves and base our concept of the Christian life on performance—the Holy Spirit will always lead us into a life that is Christ-centered.

The Holy Spirit produces fruit by joining us to the Lord and applying the work He accomplished for us on the cross: **"For the word of the cross is to those who are perishing foolishness, but to us who are being saved it is the power of God" (I Corinthians 1:18).** However, we must understand that this is the cross of Christ, not our own cross. We are called to deny ourselves and take up our crosses daily, but we are not to glory in self-abasement or try to live by the virtue of our own sacrifices. Rather, we are to glory in what Jesus accomplished and the sacrifice that *He* made (see Philippians 3:3).

We have our standing before God solely on the basis of the cross of Christ. Our ability to come boldly before the throne of God has nothing to do with whether we have had a good or a bad day, or how properly we have performed all of our religious duties. Our acceptance before God and our ability to come into His presence is based on one thing only—the sacrifice that Jesus made for our justification.

This does not negate the need for personal holiness, for as James asserted, **"Faith, if it has no works, is dead" (James 2:17).** If we are joined to Christ, we will not go on living in sin. However, we do not become free from sin in order to abide in Him, but *by* abiding in Him. Jesus is the Way, the Truth, and the Life. If He is not our Life, then we do not really know the Way or the Truth either. It is the religious spirit that tries to keep Christianity in the realm of the Way and the Truth, while keeping us from the essential union by which Jesus becomes our Life. True Christianity involves not just *what* we believe, but *Who* we believe.

True worship does not have as its purpose to see the Lord; rather, worship comes from having seen Him. When we see Him, we will worship. When we see His glory, we will no longer be captivated by our own positive or negative qualities—our souls will be captured by His beauty. When the Lamb enters, even the 24 elders will cast their crowns at His feet (Revelation 4:10). That is the goal of true faith—to see Him, to abide in Him, and to reveal Him.

The world is becoming increasingly repulsed by religion. However, when Jesus is lifted up, all men will be drawn to Him (John 12:32). Because the whole creation was created through Him and for Him, we all have a Jesus-size hole in our soul. Nothing else will ever satisfy the longing of the human heart or bring us peace, except a genuine relationship with Christ Jesus.

When we are truly joined to Jesus, unstoppable living waters begin to flow out of our innermost being. As more and more people are freed and this water begins to flow in them, it will become a great river of life in the midst of the earth. Those who drink from this river will never thirst again—they will have found satisfaction for the deepest yearning of the human soul. The more that we get free of the religious spirit, the purer and clearer these waters will be.

Special Acknowledgment

Some of the materials used in this part of the book, as well as a few of the warning signs at the end, were derived from Jack Deere's outstanding tape series *Exposing the Religious Spirit*, which is available through the Tape Catalog of *MorningStar Publications*.

The Morning Star
PROPHETIC BULLETIN

In order to swiftly promulgate important prophetic message to the Body of Christ, we have instituted this service. The primary contributors will be **Paul Cain, Rick Joyner,** and other proven prophetic ministries. **Distribution will be at irregular times dictated by the timeliness and importance of the messages received.**

Only... **$5.00!**

for a 1 year subscription!

[MSPB-001]

CALL 1-800-542-0278
TO ORDER

CREDIT CARD ORDERS ONLY